a year in the life of the langdale valleys bill birkett

FRANCES LINCOLN

a year in the life of the langdale valleys bill birkett

Many thanks
To my family – Sue, my wife; Rowan and Tamsin, my daughters; James
and William, my sons – for magical days in Langdale. To Mary Jenner
for unfailing support and Dave Birkett for his intuitive knowledge of
the fells. To the locals of the Langdales, particularly John and Maureen
Birkett, George Birkett, Melly and Marie Dixon and Neil Walmsley.
To my mates in the SOGs (Sad Old Gits), particularly Mark Squires
and George Sharpe who have never held back an opinion of my work!
To Pete Fleming and George Watkins of the Fell and Rock Climbing
Club. To Tinnie and Evelyn in Cape Town for inviting me into their
wonderful wooden home where much of this book was written. To
John Nicoll and Kate Cave of Frances Lincoln for being brave and
publishing this book. To Jane Havell for producing a fine balance of
the material. To those protective bodies and groups who care about
the Langdales and seek to protect its unique character and beauty:
the National Trust, the National Park Authority, the Countryside
Commission, English Heritage and the Friends of the Lake District.

Bill Birkett Photo Library
Bill Birkett has an extensive photographic library covering all of
Britain's mountains and wild places, including one of the most
comprehensive collections of photographs of the English Lake District.
For information, please telephone 015394 37420 or e-mail
bill.birkett1@btopenworld.com

*TITLE PAGE: A double rainbow arches over Little Langdale during
a summer shower. The bows climb over Ash Lee and Greenbank
cottages to the left and, with Little Fell behind, fall down by
Stang End and Sepulchre Wood to the right.*

Frances Lincoln Limited
4 Torriano Mews
Torriano Avenue
London NW5 2RZ

A Year in the Life of the Langdale Valleys
Copyright © 2004 Frances Lincoln Limited

Text and photographs copyright © 2004 Bill Birkett
Edited and designed by Jane Havell Associates

First Frances Lincoln edition 2004

Bill Birkett has asserted his moral right to be identified as Author of this
Work in accordance with the Copyright, Designs and Patents Act 1988

British Library cataloguing-in-publication data
A catalogue record for this book is available from
the British Library

ISBN 0-7112-2449-8

Printed in Singapore

9 8 7 6 5 4 3 2

contents

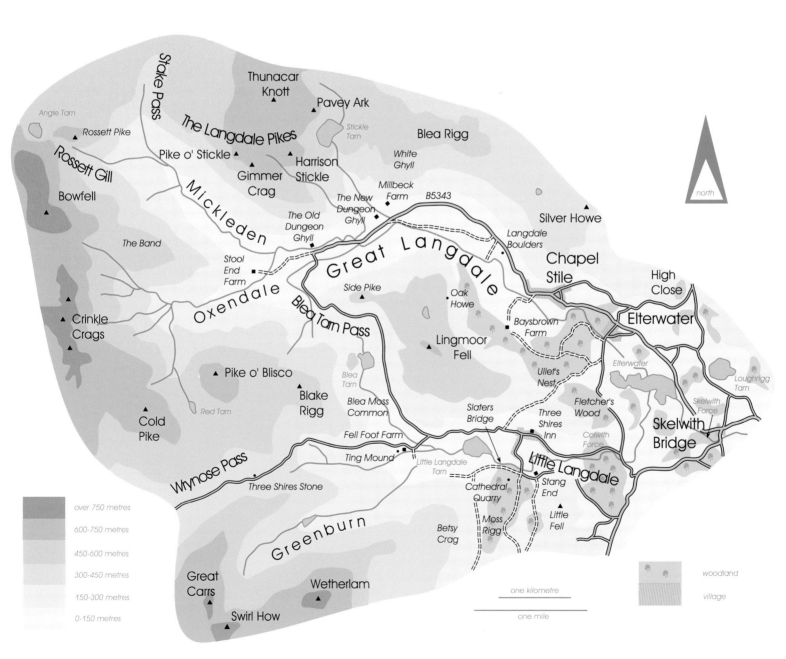

Stake Pass

Thunacar Knott

Pavey Ark

Angle Tarn

Rossett Pike

The Langdale Pikes

Stickle Tarn

Blea Rigg

Pike o' Stickle

Harrison Stickle

White Ghyll

Rossett Gill

Gimmer Crag

Millbeck Farm

B5343

Bowfell

Mickleden

The New Dungeon Ghyll

Silver Howe

The Band

The Old Dungeon Ghyll

Great Langdale

Langdale Boulders

Chapel Stile

High Close

Stool End Farm

Side Pike

Oak Howe

Baysbrown Farm

Elterwater

Oxendale

Blea Tarn Pass

Crinkle Crags

Lingmoor Fell

Ullet's Nest

Elterwater

Loughrigg Tarn

Pike o' Blisco

Blea Tarn

Fletcher's Wood

Cold Pike

Blake Rigg

Red Tarn

Blea Moss Common

Slaters Bridge

Three Shires Inn

Colwith Force

Skelwith Bridge

Fell Foot Farm

Ting Mound

Little Langdale Tarn

Little Langdale

Skelwith Force

Wrynose Pass

Three Shires Stone

Cathedral Quarry

Stang End

Little Fell

Greenburn

Betsy Crag

Moss Rigg

Great Carrs

Wetherlam

Swirl How

north

Legend:

over 750 metres
600-750 metres
450-600 metres
300-450 metres
150-300 metres
0-150 metres

woodland

village

one kilometre

one mile

Knobbly tops and round bottoms – the Langdales. My home, the best place on earth. When you love something so much – when it has been with you all your life and you have felt the pain of each winter, the hope of each spring, the warmth of summer and the magic of autumn – how do you describe it in a few words, where do you start? For me the best way of communicating a little of its natural wonder, its nooks and crannies, history and pastimes, and my passion for them is through my photography. But first, here is an attempt to place the Langdale valleys in some kind of context.

In Old Norse, Langdale simply means 'long valley'. There are actually two valleys, Great and Little Langdale, one quite long and the other a bit shorter, in the north-west of England within Britain's largest National Park – the Lake District. Lakeland has long inspired artists, poets, photographers, walkers and climbers. Its fells (mountains), lakes and tarns (little lakes high in the fells), trees and valleys combine to create one of the most sublimely beautiful landscapes in the world.

Cutting deep into the mountains and separated by Lingmoor Fell, the Langdales form two contrasting dales. Soaring from green fields, Great Langdale presents the stark rugged grandeur of the Pikes, England's best-known mountain outline, set against the might of Crinkle Crags and Bowfell. Whatever the season, when the clouds are not piled too thick, its skyline cannot fail to impress. Little Langdale is subtler: its mixed woods guard many secrets before it opens to village and tarn to reveal the magnificence of Wetherlam and Great Carrs, an aspect that looks almost Himalayan when plastered white with the snows of winter.

Set almost in the centre of the Lake District, the Langdales run westwards from the plains feeding into the head of Lake Windermere. Many visitors will get their first tantalising glimpse of Wetherlam, Lingmoor Fell and the reclining lion shape of the Pikes while driving along the shores of Windermere. It is their unique scale and perfection of proportion that make the Langdales so special – the juxtaposition of fell, farm, tarn, tree, stone wall and field. Everything, including the signs of human intrusion, fits in harmony. That is quite astonishing considering that industry – production of the stone axe on a grand scale – started among the Langdale Pikes some seven thousand years ago. More of this later. First of all, to familiarise you with the basic layout of the valleys I will take you on a brief tour.

Great Langdale
Our starting point is Skelwith Bridge, which marks the foot of the Great Langdale valley. From here the road leads above Skelwith Force towards Elterwater lake. A look down from the road reveals the path below, following along the old water conduit that once powered the water wheels at Skelwith Bridge. A handrail and a little bridge lead to the flat rock top of the falls. The banks of the River Brathay are a delight, with deep pools cutting lazily through the meadows from the foot of the lake. Rob Rash Wood follows, with the steep hillside above falling from the fell of Little Loughrigg. Over the top of the fell and hidden behind lies the quiet jewel of Loughrigg Tarn.

Elterwater consists of three basins and is quite unusual. You can't really appreciate its complexities from the banks; you need to scale the heights of Lingmoor or Loughrigg for these to be revealed. From low down it's a sylvan scene with mixed woods, rising through Fletcher's Wood to Little Langdale and up on to the end of Lingmoor Fell. Along the road you pass over a cattle grid and it begins to feel like real mountain Langdale, with a fine view to the Pikes. The Neddy Boggle Stone, a milestone with a haunted history, marks a split – left into the stone hamlet of Elterwater with its maple tree, bowling green and inn, or right over Elterwater Common into the confines of the valley and to the sublime fells. I always feel a rush of excitement at this point. The hills are calling.

Woods line both sides of the road. Mainly hidden on the left stands a timeshare development in the grounds of an old

gunpowder works. The scene opens out and the river touches the roadside before we enter Chapel Stile village, capital of the Langdales, with an inn, gala field, Co-op plus café, school, church and graveyard. My children asked me the other day whether I wanted to be burnt or buried. Despite Viking tradition, I have an inkling that the peace of Chapel Stile graveyard will do very nicely.

On leaving the village, access to Baysbrown Farm campsite lies to the left. Above this point the valley takes on an S-shape and deepens as the heights begin to unfold. A deeply pocketed stone stands above the road before low iron railings to the left offer a breathtaking view over Langdale Boulders to the Pikes. Neolithic man must have appreciated this scene too, once he had chopped the trees down: he left his mark on the boulders to emphasise the point. The flat fields of the valley bottom contrast markedly with the steep flanks of the fells on either side.

We pass numerous farms, houses and climbing huts and a caravan site (above the road and masked by trees) before, at the top of a slight rise, a lone stone barn marks the point at which many climbers leave the valley floor for sunny Scout Crag or the formidable steeps of White Ghyll. Down the hill we pass the drive that leads up to Millbeck Farm, properly known as Low Millbeck, before arriving at the New Dungeon Ghyll Hotel. This is a 'modern' addition to the valley – built in 1862! Two large car parks mark this as the main walkers' access point to the Pikes. Harrison Stickle stands high to the north of the road while the craggy knoll opposite is Side Pike, the terminus of Lingmoor Fell which has formed the left side of the valley to this point.

A little further on, past the campsite to the left, is the Old Dungeon Ghyll Hotel and a third car park. Immediately above we can see Raven Crag – spot the climbers. At the point where the road turns left is a gate: the track beyond (no public access for cars) leads straight ahead to Stool End Farm, nestling at the

LEFT: Skelwith Force waterfall lies just beyond the hamlet of Skelwith Bridge on the river which is now the Brathay (pronounced 'bray-thee'). In times of spate a formidable amount of water plunges over this drop – this barrier prevents migrating salmon from spawning in the Langdales. The waterfall has been tapped for many centuries for energy to power water wheels.

foot of The Band. The Band is the spur that falls from the Three Tarns Col just below Bowfell, effectively separating the two heads of Great Langdale. Oxendale lies to its left, and the long flat-bottomed valley of Mickleden to the right. Left of Oxendale stand the plucky heights of Pike o' Blisco while arrayed to the right, over the hollow of Red Tarn, is the serrated outline of Crinkle Crags. Mickleden reaches on beneath Bowfell to the south west and Pike o' Stickle to the north up to the rocky faces of Rossett Pike, Buck Pike and Black Crags. At this point, Stake Pass, the high walkers' path to Borrowdale, rises to the right. An old packhorse route by Rossett Gill climbs to the left, leading to Angle Tarn and the mountain crossroads of Esk Hause.

Our road now makes a ninety-degree turn to the left and starts to climb steeply up to Blea Tarn Pass, winding over and down into the head of Little Langdale.

Little Langdale

South of Lingmoor Fell, Little Langdale rises steeply from Low Colwith Farm. Halfway up the first hill, a peek through the woods on the left side of the road reveals a vertical drop of some 20 metres (60 feet) directly into the River Brathay, which once divided the valley into Lancashire and Westmorland. Just upstream is the tumbling cascade of Colwith Force waterfall. The woods here, wild and populated by both roe and red deer, were coppiced in the seventeenth century to make charcoal for the iron industry.

The first building, below to the left, is Hacket Forge. Locally it is called Force Forge, which is exactly what it was four hundred years ago – the centre of an important iron industry then at the cutting edge of technology. The road rises to offer a fine view across the valley bottom over the cottages of Fitz Steps to mighty Wetherlam. A cottage facing us, on the end of a row of slate cottages, was once Greenbank Farm, built by the infamous Lanty Slee, distiller of illicit whiskey. We pass Greenbank and enter the village of Little Langdale with the Three

Shires Inn at its centre. Just beyond the inn, above a telephone box, there is limited parking.

A road down to the left crosses a ford and follows a secretive wooded valley, cutting through to Tilberthwaite and eventually on to Coniston. Atkinson Coppice woods overlook the river and the area is thick with the slate spoil from disused quarries, including the striking Cathedral Quarry. South of Little Langdale valley are Little Fell and Holme Fell. The track to Tilberthwaite separates these from the tops, which rise progressively to the serene bulk of Wetherlam.

Continuing up the main road, we come to a crossroads at the top of the hill. Left, for walkers only, leads to Slaters Bridge; right becomes the Ullets Nest track to Great Langdale. Further

ABOVE: Perched on the steep bank at the entrance to Little Langdale village, Greenbank Farm was built in 1840 by Lanty Slee, a notorious distiller of illicit whiskey. It was the last farm to be built in the Langdales.

on down the hill lies Little Langdale Tarn – although perfectly visible from the road it has no public access, and under the guardianship of George and John Birkett it has become a haven for wildlife. Across the tarn are the picturesque former farm-steads of Low and High Hallgarth; above, the hanging valley of Greenburn separates Wetherlam from Wetside Edge above Wrynose Pass. Around the head of the pass are Swirl How and Great and Little Carrs. The road rises to wind around a rocky knoll. A strip of smooth rock slab that goes directly over the top is known as 'the Roman road' and probably is. Busk Farm is on the right before a slight ascent and descent lead to a cattle grid.

The road to the right climbs to Blea Tarn and thence down to Great Langdale. West of Blea Tarn are Blake Rigg and Pike o' Blisco, while the craggy, brackened slopes of Lingmoor Fell run the full length of the valley on the right. The left fork takes us on past Fell Foot Farm, with its secret porch at the front leading directly on to the road – this is where Lanty Slee's illicit whiskey was despatched. At the back of the farm stands Ting Mound, the site of the Viking parliament. The road now rises to climb Wrynose Pass, steepening dramatically before levelling and continuing to the Three Shires Stone, which marks the meeting place of the old counties of Lancashire, Westmorland and Cumberland. Beyond this point the road falls to Wrynose Bottom and the head of the Duddon valley.

winter

This is the time for the land to rest. Howling westerlies blow clouds of spindrift from the heights. Traditionally farmers use their stockpile of summer hay and the beasts stay in barns, while the Herdwick sheep are brought down from the high fells to lower pastures. Redwing and field-fare, geese and whooper swan appear from the Arctic north, looking for the good life in Lakeland. The winter mountaineer looks for consolidated snow and frozen waterfalls to climb. The walker enjoys blue skies and clear mountain vistas.

OPPOSITE: Over the deep pool of Rob's Hole (pronounced 'robs-el'), frost and mist grip the larch woods by Little Langdale Tarn. Winter's snows will soon be arriving. This photograph was taken from a favourite viewpoint on the path dropping from Birk Howe to Slaters Bridge.

OVERLEAF: A moody sunrise in Little Langdale heralds a cold winter's day. Snow has fallen during the night and lingering cloud suggests there may be more to follow. 'Red sky in the morning, shepherd's warning' – but in the mountains who knows what the day will bring?

OPPOSITE TOP: Spanning soft ground and rock outcrop alike, many dry stone walls look like ramshackle affairs. But they are built to a very ingenious design: double-skinned with a rubble-filled core, their construction allows them to behave plastically when the ground underfoot settles. While they may take on some funny shapes and bulges, they seldom fall down.

OPPOSITE: I call this the 'Great Wall of China'. Dividing Little from Great Langdale, it runs along the very spine of Lingmoor near Brown Howe. It is a particularly fine example of the art of dry stone walling, with top and bottom level 'through stones' at regular intervals and 'cam stones', which change the direction of the slope, at each peak and each hollow.

RIGHT: The north-west face of Gimmer Crag forms a 100-metre (300-feet) bastion, sweeping up elegantly from the steep fellside. Fine-grained red and white volcanic rock amplify the pale yellow light of a winter sun to produce a warming gold-brown.

ABOVE: A Herdwick ewe grazes on Lingmoor Fell against the dramatic backdrop of the Pikes. Over the fence, on the Great Langdale side, the ground is clad with heather – the 'ling' of Lingmoor – while on the Little Langdale side it is grassier and more suitable for grazing.

ABOVE: Herdwick tup rams strut their thing. George Birkett calls them 'tips' and he should know – they are his. Red dye, known as 'smit', is smeared at the front end of a tup ram, so that ewes that have stood to the ram can be identified by the red mark on their backs.

LEFT: A mute swan by the foot of Elterwater, with this season's cygnets behind as evidence that the swans are resident year round. The name Elterwater, from Old Norse, means 'swan lake'. Keep an eye on your sandwiches if you sit on the bench here!

OPPOSITE: Above Skelwith Bridge at the foot of the Langdales, Loughrigg Tarn occupies an elevated position between the fells of Loughrigg and Little Loughrigg. This aspect, looking towards Wetherlam, the high fell that dominates Little Langdale, shows a perfection of scale – tree, lake, cottage and mountain. The cottage reflected in the gently rippling waters is known as Crag Head.

OVERLEAF: As evening gathers over Bowfell, with no one else on the mountain the quiet is so intense it is deafening. This aspect looks towards the summit from the northern shoulder.

LEFT: In Little Langdale winter sun breaks through the enchanting oak woods on the track beyond the ford that crosses the River Brathay. The track skirts round a high tree-clad knoll to cross a stone-arched bridge and climb to Stang End. A stone hen-hut once stood on the shoulder of the knoll and I used to collect the eggs for Fred Bowness.

LEFT: Witch tree by the track above Loughrigg Tarn. This is a tree from which another tree grows – here, a fir grows on an ancient pollarded ash. In Celtic mythology, the 'guest' tree was thought to have magical properties and was used to make Druids' wands. It is not attached to the earth, nor has it moved to the world beyond – it occupies the magical middle kingdom. Pollarded ash trees, their top branches cut on a regular seasonal basis, are a major feature of the Langdales. Their ancient trunks may be completely hollow – indeed, a whole side of their bole may be missing – but they live on.

BELOW: Delicate early morning frost brings a holly leaf into sharp relief. A few moments later, the rising sun will have melted all traces of this winter artistry. Traditionally, the waxy green leaves and red berries of the prickly holly form an important part of Christmas cheer. Its straight branches were used to make walking sticks of distinction – I have my grandfather's favourite self-made holly stick in front of me as I write this.

ABOVE: Whorneyside Force at the head of Oxendale has been blasted by a bitterly cold easterly wind which has transformed the waterfall into ice. Three main becks feed into Oxendale: Browney Gill, rising from Red Tarn, tumbles to the left; Crinkle Gill falls centrally direct from Crinkle Crags, and Whorneyside Force comes from the direction of Three Tarns via the deep rift of Hell Gill.

OPPOSITE: Looking from Broad Slack to the Carrs, with the Scafell Massif behind. To the discerning mountaineer's eye this cold and lonely scene well portrays the mechanics of snow and ice formation on the heights, and forewarns of considerable winter dangers. Snow stripped to reveal bare ground shows that strong westerlies, accelerated to high velocities over the col, have built cornices on the east face and deposited unstable soft snow in the gully below. Cornices collapse – keep back from the edge. Unconsolidated snow avalanches – keep out of the gullies. Wind-glazed ground and ice may be so hard that even the sharpest crampon points will not bite – have your ice axe ready to arrest a fall.

BELOW: Ice on Red Tarn – with the view over to Bowfell it looks delectable, but it is certainly below zero out there. The tarn's name comes from the hematite that once coloured the waters red in the days when the iron ore industry flourished here – mines were sunk around the tarn and down Browney Gill.

OPPOSITE: Winter reflections in Blea Tarn allow the Pikes, including Side Pike, to be seen twice in one viewing.

ABOVE: Seen from Wetside
Edge, a blanket of snow covers
Wetherlam above Little Langdale.
In the hollow below lies the
hanging valley Greenburn,
once mined for copper.

ABOVE: A mighty view across the head of the Langdales from the spine of Lingmoor Fell: on the left rises Pike o' Blisco, followed by Crinkle Crags, with Bowfell to the right. Lingmoor Fell provides perhaps the finest views of the high mountains.

ABOVE: All that glitters is gold –
winter sunset over Three Tarns
seen from Pike o' Stickle. The
dark fellside climbing to the
right is the shoulder of Bowfell.

ABOVE: The great rocky head of Pike o' Stickle looks out at the sun setting over Allen Crags between Great End (left) and Great Gable (right). It was on these heights that Neolithic man quarried volcanic tuff to make his stone axes; the evidence of something like 3,000 years of industrial activity remains in the form of caves and chipping sites. The summit can only be reached by a rough scramble but the view from the top more than repays the effort.

climbing

Great Langdale is one of the most famous locations in Britain for rock climbing. It abounds with steep rocks and great routes, and climbers have been enjoying these virtues for over a hundred years. My father, Jim Birkett, was a great pioneer of difficult routes: in the 1930s and 1940s he opened climbs that were at the time some of the hardest ever made. My nephew, Dave Birkett, has recently taken on the role and in between I also made a contribution. So I think it's fair to say that rock is in our blood!

OPPOSITE TOP LEFT: Ice climbing on Whorneyside Force: a climber equipped with crampons and ice axes enjoys the winter transformation of this lovely waterfall.

OPPOSITE BOTTOM LEFT: The rough-pocketed rock on the East Wall of Pavey Ark is ideal for climbing – but it requires strong fingers and a head for heights. Here, my nephew Dave Birkett returns to a route on which he made the first-ever ascent, one of the most difficult rock climbs in Britain. Never mind the climbing – getting the photograph was difficult enough!

OPPOSITE RIGHT: Tim Emmet makes an accomplished and stylish second ascent of the extremely difficult 'Dawes Rides a Shovel Head', another Dave Birkett route, on Raven Crag immediately behind the Old Dungeon Ghyll Hotel. I've climbed here myself and, incidentally, taught Dave all he knows about climbing – and he still knows nothing!

RIGHT: High above Mickleden, Tansy Hardy climbs Jim Birkett's North West Arete on Gimmer Crag – one of the great routes of the region. The clean faces of Gimmer, its steep cracks and corners and stepped overhangs present a challenge to each generation's most talented rock climbers. Many have left their mark here with daring first ascents: R. B. Reynolds climbed The Crack in 1928; ace South African R. V. M. Barry took very steep ground on his Groove's Traverse in 1936; Jim Birkett added pure magic with North West Arete and F Route in 1940, and the great A. R. Dolphin added the ferocious Kipling Groove (so called because it was 'ruddy hard') in 1948.

volcanoes, flora and fauna

Geology

Look at the Langdale rocks over any small area and you will find lots of very different formations, from fist-sized knobbly bits sticking out of gritty boulders to smooth, flat, slate slabs. Once, not long ago, these were labelled tuffs (from fine-grained flinty ashes) or andesites and rhyolites (from lavas). The classification has recently been broadened to recognise thick lavas, ignimbrites and tuffs. The most significant influence on the formation of all these rocks was the volcanic mayhem that erupted some 440 million years ago, around the end of the Ordovician period. The rocks thus formed are known as the Borrowdale volcanics. (That's mistake number one by the geologists – anyone can see that they should really be called the Langdale volcanics. Imagine all the sensitive, gentle people of Langdale having to live with this ignominy!)

Modern geologists are only just beginning to interpret what went on in the complex period during which these rocks were formed. It's easy to imagine Mount Fuji-type volcanoes spewing out molten rock and lava into symmetrical cone-shaped mounds, but that would be a simplification. There were also huge explosions, like the ones that blew apart Krakatoa and Mount St Helens, and vast crater lakes, undermined by soft molten magma, which simply collapsed downwards. The Langdale rocks were formed from flowing lava, from bubbles and pipes of underground magma emerging from the depths, from molten bombs thrown through the air, from ash that settled through crater lakes.

When the volcanoes fell silent, more happened. Seas rose and fell, covering and uncovering the mountains; more than once, the land was lifted and folded, stressing and fracturing the rocks. Water eroded the mountains to produce a pattern of V-shaped valleys. In the meantime, hot molten magmas rose to form new rocks, with hot gases and hydrothermal veins to metamorphose and mineralise. Finally there came a hundred and fifty thousand or so years of Ice Age and glaciation. The

flow of ice produced the deep U-shaped valley of Great Langdale – a classic feature of glaciation – and left the rocky tops and hanging corries and tarns that so much influence the landscape we see today.

Some of these geological processes produced rocks and minerals so desirable to man that their use transformed the landscape. Silicon-rich fine-grained andesite tuffs have a property known as conchoidal fracture – in other words, when struck with a tougher rock (granite will do nicely) the tuff chips to leave a dish-shaped hollow and a curved flake with an edge that can be worked to razor sharpness. In Neolithic times, from around 2,000 to 5,000 BC, these rocks were used to produce stone axes. With these the valleys were cleared of trees and farming began.

Lumps of fractured rock meant there was a plentiful supply of material for the stone walls that are a major feature of both valleys. There are also deposits of copper and iron, mined since the Bronze Age (c. 2,000 BC), with copper deposits stretching from Tilberthwaite Gill over Birk Fell and Betsy Crag to Greenburn. Some types of fine-grained tuff will split into straight slabs when struck with a hammer and chisel. This is slate – and it makes perfect roofing material, as witnessed by all the buildings in the area using this attractive light- to olive-green stone. The Romans were probably the first to use slate slabs produced like this; latterly they have been chosen for facing material for Coventry Cathedral and many other prestigious buildings at home and abroad. Slate quarrying has been a major influence on both the economy and the landscape of the Langdales.

Plants and wildlife

Juniper and arctic birch were among the first trees to colonise the uplands once the ice began to melt. Interestingly, the juniper is still prevalent, a living descendant of the original shrub, found here for eleven thousand years. Pine, willow and alder followed and then oak forests which grew to a height of 750 metres (2,500 feet). Animals including wolves, elk and bears arrived as the climate became warmer.

Around seven thousand years ago, farming began to change the face of the Langdales. Under the influence of grazing and fire, dwarf shrub heaths were replaced by acidic grasslands and bracken. The process has accelerated over the last two hundred years, with flora and fauna becoming markedly altered. Within the last sixty years, modern farming methods, which rely on heavy machinery and the use of chemicals, have led to a serious deterioration of wildlife habitats across the whole farmland scene.

That apart, to the layman's eye a wealth of plant and wild life still flourishes in the dales and on the tops. Birch, sycamore, ash, oak, hazel, rowan, yew and pine trees are to be seen and the variation of colour in bracken and on fellside through the seasons is one of the region's most attractive features.

In the air and on the Langdale crags there are peregrine, raven, buzzard, ring ouzel and a host of smaller birds. These can all still be seen in a single day here. In April the valleys are alive with the sound of the cuckoo. In summer the farmhouses and cottages are graced with swallow, swift and house martin.

On the ground red fox, hare, rabbit, roe and red deer, hedgehog and badger are relatively common. You may see an occasional stoat or weasel. The otter is elusive, but survives. Tragically, in a matter of only a few years, the indigenous red squirrel has virtually disappeared, ousted by the grey. The pine martin, once seen occasionally in Little Langdale, has also gone. Local rarities include a white red deer hind, and white moles as captured by master mole-catcher Ed Birkett. Of the wrigglies, slow-worm are a relatively frequent sight but the adder has become increasingly thin on the ground.

On the water, great crested grebe, greylag goose (also to be seen grazing in the fields), goosander and black-headed gull are now regulars. Under the water, sticklebacks, frogs, minnows and brown trout, though much scarcer now then when I was a boy, are seen in both beck and tarn. Pike and perch accompany the brown trout in Elterwater and Loughrigg Tarn.

OPPOSITE: Grey-blue spoil heaps from disused slate quarries form a substantial part of the Langdales landscape, and bear testimony to the importance of a once flourishing industry. These banks of waste slate are from the Cathedral Quarry complex in Atkinson Coppice, Little Langdale. Silver birch and larch, self-planted, are slowly reclaiming them for nature.

spring

Life begins again after the dark and cold of winter. Raven, peregrine and buzzard are all with chick. A host of flowers appears in the woods and around the verges and riverbanks as if by magic. It's lambing time for the farmers and groups of lambs begin to gambol in the fields – a heartwarming sight. A variety of blossom colours the scene and the bracken starts to unfurl its green head through the dead remnants of last year's growth. The call of the cuckoo lifts the spirits. When I was a child we all used to dance around the maypole at Chapel Stile. Rock climbers practise on the Boulders with huge ambitions for the forthcoming sunshine.

OPPOSITE: A favourite garden tree throughout both valleys is undoubtably the cherry. Its lovely white-pink blossom emerges in April to lift spirits sullied by the long, cold nights of winter.

OPPOSITE: Disturbed from its grazing, this little roe deer makes a rapid escape to leap over the stone wall in one easy bound. Possibly due to the demise of 'country ways' – hunting and poaching – both red and roe deer abound in the woods adjoining the valleys. While gardeners may complain about damage to their shrubs, most people delight in the sight of these graceful, placid creatures.

BELOW: Spring sunshine at Little Langdale streams through to unfurl the delicate leaves of the silver birch – undoubtedly one of the prettiest trees of mountain and lake country.

OVERLEAF: Across the dale and meadows of Little Langdale winter loses its grip, with life and colour miraculously appearing again. The tired brown grass of winter becomes green, new-born lambs follow their mothers and the bony fingers of the winter trees begin to soften and colour.

ABOVE: Beautifully situated to keep an eye on the young lambs, this traditional farmhouse and its adjoining stone barn look out across the meadows near the top of Red Bank, the point where Great Langdale falls to Grasmere.

ABOVE: Following the yellow of
the daffodils in March and early
April come the bluebells in May.
Wood and hillside alike are
carpeted in bright blue.

LEFT: The deep, secretive cleft of Dungeon Ghyll rises from the valley floor, near the New Dungeon Ghyll car park, to cut beneath Pike How and emerge into the open before once more diving into the depths of the mountain between Thorn Crag and Pike o' Stickle. There are a number of cascading waterfalls en route – this is the most visible, easily seen from the footpath that leads from the car park via Mark Gate to Loft Crag. The ghyll takes its name from the main waterfall, out of sight, which drops just downstream. At this point the water has cut deep into the rock to form a narrow chasm which can only be reached by scrambling over boulders and rock outcrops. The fall is some 20 metres (70 feet), and the roof of the chasm is choked by a huge boulder spanning the cleft – so once you enter the final amphitheatre to view the fall it really feels as if you are enclosed in some subterranean dungeon.

OPPOSITE: Stood on an ancient stone wall made from huge blocks that have tumbled down the scree below Raven Crag, a male yellowhammer with its vivid yellow breast contrasts markedly with a black and threatening sky. This lane, lined by stone walls, makes a high connection between the Old Dungeon Ghyll and the New Dungeon Ghyll hotels.

OVERLEAF: Harrison Stickle, Pike o' Stickle and Loft Crag profiled against the pink sky of a magical spring evening. A long lens emphasises the subtle graduation of light on the falling ridges, and so captures the depth of the Great Langdale valley. This viewpoint is on the hillside just above High Close.

ABOVE: Beyond a great larch, radiant in the sunshine, cherry blossom takes pride of place above High Colwith Farm, Little Langdale.

ABOVE: One of the great features of spring in the Langdales is the bursting forth of white blossom from gnarly old thorn trees. The blackthorn seen here, hawthorn and whitethorn all contribute. In a good year, individual trees suddenly hang thick with blossom to transform whole hillsides, which look as though they have suffered a freak snowstorm.

OPPOSITE: Above the footpath through Rob Rash Wood, by the shores of Elterwater, a wild cherry beats all other contenders to blossom first.

ABOVE: The pied wagtail – seen here at Elterwater – is a bird for all seasons. In springtime, however, its numbers seem to increase sharply. Its rapid nervous fluttering flight and vigorous tail-wagging radiate energy.

OPPOSITE TOP LEFT: The white sparkling stars of the wood anemone appear on the banks and beneath the trees.

OPPOSITE TOP RIGHT: The unmistakable cultivated yellow daffodil, probably the region's most famous flower, is found throughout the valleys. The smaller indigenous Lakeland daffodil can also still be found growing wild through various sections of woodland. Do not pick these flowers or indeed any wild flowers – they are in decline and their survival is under threat.

OPPOSITE BOTTOM LEFT: Probably the most welcome of all the springtime flowers, the wild primrose radiates the promise of warmth and sunshine to follow. Posies of primrose suddenly emerge from the leaf litter of the woods and from the sheltered river banks, announcing that winter has ended.

OPPOSITE BOTTOM RIGHT: In early June the pinks and whites of the wild climbing rose grace the hedgerows, to return as blood-red hips in autumn.

RIGHT: The walk by the River Brathay from Skelwith to Elterwater is resplendent in its variety of trees; it is a good outing to view the delights of the seasons.

LEFT: Cathedral Quarry, in Atkinson Coppice between the ford over the River Brathay in Little Langdale and Slaters Bridge, is a complex of disused slate quarries. Originally it started with a tunnel leading into a sop of what quarrymen call 'good metal', which was extracted to form a huge underground chamber, a 'close head'. This stone pillar was left in place to support the roof. As work progressed, further tunnels were driven into the chamber, allowing natural daylight to flood in and illuminate the awe-inspiring underground architecture.

OPPOSITE: A watery sun drops over the shoulder of Lingmoor, its light reflected from the rippled surface of Elterwater through the as yet leafless oaks of Rob Rash.

ABOVE: From the southern side of Little Langdale Tarn a wild aspect is revealed. Willow, silver birch and even some of the oaks are responding to the May sunshine and beginning to unfurl their leaves. The high rocky crag in the centre is Blake Rigg; the distinctive knoll beyond the tarn to the left, with Wrynose Pass beginning its winding ascent, is Castle Howe. An old iron mooring ring fastened in the rock behind this point suggests that the tarn's waters once extended further than they do now.

ABOVE: Greylag geese swim by on their exit from Elterwater to graze the meadows by the meandering pools of the River Brathay. These handsome birds now nest and breed in the Lake District, but in my childhood they were a rarity and did not nest south of the Scottish border. I remember with some amusement when they first nested on an island in the Lakes: my father, on a bitterly cold April day, stripped off to swim out to them. He didn't quite make it – and turned round with a hint of desperation to reach the safety of the shore once again, shivering and rather blue in colour. His entreaties that I should wear my jacket on a cold day lost a lot of authority after that!

RIGHT: Grazing contentedly in the meadows, greylag geese seem quite happy to mix with sheep and are not overtly nervous with people. Their recent breeding in the Lakes is a wildlife success story.

OPPOSITE: May blossom in the Langdales creates a heady mix of fragrances. Typical examples are hawthorn (top left), blackthorn (top and bottom right) and cultivated cherry (bottom left).

BELOW: High on Colwith Brow above the foot of Little Langdale a shaft of light from the falling sun breaks through the cloud to awaken the colours of early spring. Once this area would have been coppiced with hazel, ash and birch to provide fuel for the charcoal-burners who supplied the iron-smelting industry at Colwith Force and Hacket (Force) Forge.

farming

OPPOSITE: Hay time in Little Langdale in the fields belonging to Wilson Place Farm. The hay is being turned into rolls to dry in the summer sunshine.

BELOW: Dale End Farm, with spring sunshine drying the washing, marks the start of the stony Ullets Nest track over to Great Langdale. It is therefore the end of the dale for travellers. In descent the track forks to enter the villages of Chapel Stile and Elterwater. When I was a lad we regularly used to travel this route by motorbike and sidecar and, though hard to believe, it is still classified as a public road.

the human imprint

First to make a permanent impact on the scene after the big freeze was Neolithic man, who started operations around 5,000 BC. He invented and perfected the Langdale stone axe, cleared trees from the valleys and started farming. In the Pikes, axe production went on for some two thousand years or more – the chippings are reputed to have produced the bulk of the Great Stone Shoot which runs from the side of Pike o' Stickle virtually to the floor of Mickleden. Only 'roughings' were produced here: they were transported to the coast for finishing and polishing. Apart from the functionality of these axes – their razor edges are actually sharper than steel – they are objects of considerable beauty. They were traded all over Britain and I have heard it reported that axes from Langdale have been found on the Continent. If so, Langdale had its own export trade some seven thousand years ago!

Neolithic man left another indelible mark on the landscape: the 'rock art' on the Langdale Boulders. Here is a system of concentric circles, each circle with a short line feathered across it at right angles, connected by straight-line grooves. There are other shapes and markings, too. Is this random image-making? Does it tell a story? Is it some kind of language? As yet no one has the answers. One thing I am certain of is that these markings were extremely important to the society that made them. They are precision etchings into very hard rhyolite and they were executed before the invention of metal. Try cutting Langdale volcanics even with a hard steel chisel – it isn't easy. Society at that time must surely have been preoccupied with survival, yet some person or group of skilled people were allotted a significant amount of time to make these marks. (Because I climbed regularly on the Langdale Boulders and built up knowledge of the site over the years, I photographed these etchings before they were officially accredited. Within the valley I know of two further sites, unrecorded to date, with markings that I suspect may be contemporaneous. Curiously, the markings at each site are completely different.)

Mining of both copper and iron ore, red hematite, may have begun during the Bronze and Iron Ages. Hut circles and burial mounds from this period abound throughout the flat bottom of Mickleden and on the humps of moraine and the drumlins (the ridges left by glaciers) beneath Rossett Gill and Stake Pass. Classic features of Bronze Age farmsteads can be seen at sites near present-day farms – for example, the walled lanes that run from behind Millbeck and alongside Wall End in Great Langdale. Evidence of settlement can also be found on the mound behind Oak Howe. On Blea Moss are the remains of what locals call the 'stone circle': this resembles a walled enclosure rather than the more commonly accepted form of circle.

The Romans turned up around 75 AD and stayed for something like three hundred years. They built a road over Wrynose, from Hardknott Fort through Little Langdale to the fort at Ambleside. This was a main west-to-east route connecting the port at Ravenglass to Penrith via the high pass of High Street. A few signs remain of the most probable route through the dale. The most obvious is what locals call 'the Roman road', which takes a direct line over the summit of a glaciated rocky knoll (roche moutonnée) near the head of Little Langdale Tarn.

When Roman influence waned, the Celtic tribes and the Romano-British – collectively known as 'the Cymry' – held sway. Hence the name given by the Anglo-Saxon Chronicle to the north-west corner of England and the lands stretching over the Solway to Strathclyde: 'Cumbraland'.

Somewhere around the eighth century, the Vikings arrived. They came as raiders and stayed on as settlers and farmers, and had a profound effect on the region and on its place names. The name Langdale is pure Old Norse; so are fell (from fjall), tarn (from tjorn), beck (from bekkr), and almost all the names in the Langdales. My surname comes from the Viking name Bjork.

Under the Normans, the establishment of Furness Abbey had a major impact on the Langdales. The monks organised farming and exploitation of the considerable natural mineral

wealth of the area. Hematite from Ore Gap, between Bowfell and Esk Pike, was mined. The monks established the wool trade, produced charcoal and smelted iron.

Some time in the seventeenth century, mining took off in a much bigger way. Copper was won from Greenburn, above Little Langdale. Hematite was taken from Red Tarn, beneath Pike o' Blisco. Little Langdale became an important site for producing iron – Hacket Forge, known locally as Force Forge, and Colwith Force were major areas of production. Water power was used to turn wheels which activated bellows to force air into the furnaces – forerunners of Bessemer's blast furnace. Local coppices supplied wood for charcoal, a key ingredient in the production process. Many of the farms in the Langdale valleys were built during this period, and look almost unchanged to this day.

In the eighteenth century, slate quarrying became more extensive; in many cases the activity was centred on small farms where it supplemented or replaced a farming income. A rich vein of slate, containing good 'mettle', runs north-east through the Langdales from Tilberthwaite and Lingmoor to Thrang Quarry, immediately above Chapel Stile. There is a maze of workings, underground and surface, and associated trackways and buildings. The Enclosures Act of 1801 apportioned common land and open fields to those who could afford to enclose it by a certain date. Those who could not build a wall around their land lost their ancient common rights. Huge changes followed, notably the considerable increase of drystone walls over the fells and in the dales. Whole families built these walls, sleeping out on the fell to resume work early the next morning. Some walls are works of art in their own right and stand to this day, a testimony to the wallers' craft and skill. Agriculture changed dramatically: farmers improved the soils of the newly enclosed fields with lime and with heavy applications of manure. Wetlands were drained so that what had once been bog with willow and alder became green fertile field.

Rough fell slopes were also enclosed and known as intakes (pronounced 'in-taks'). They were smoothed over by cutting the heather, bracken and heath and burning the stubble. The land was more extensively ploughed and stock levels increased significantly.

In the nineteenth century many of the smaller farmsteads were abandoned. But some farmers bucked the trend: the last farm in the Langdales – Greenbank Farm in Little Langdale – was built in 1840 by one Lanty Slee. Officially he was a quarryman but it was common knowledge that his wealth came from the illicit distillation of whiskey. The remains of his stills can be found around Little Langdale in three main sites. The best known is in the long quarry scar that rises above the valley towards Betsy Crag. It is well hidden behind a stone wall that masks the entrance to an abandoned quarry tunnel; until the 1960s, when unfortunately it was vandalised, Lanty's hearth, various vessels and empty barrels could all be seen much as he had left them over a century before.

Bobbin mills operated wherever there were waterfalls powerful enough to turn the water wheels. Skelwith Force was a prime site, with Jeremiah Coward's mill operating downstream at Skelwith Bridge. Similarly powered, by water running along a sluice leading from a weir in Langdale Beck, the Elterwater Gunpowder Works opened in 1824; in 1838 Stickle Tarn beneath Pavey Ark was dammed to supplement the water supply should the beck run dry. In the 1890s the works employed 80 people, known locally as 'powder monkeys'; it continued to operate until 1929. In 1894 the number of pupils at Chapel Stile School averaged 120, with a further 50 in Little Langdale and a similar number at Skelwith Bridge. Today only two working slate quarries remain, Elterwater and Betsy Crag. Little Langdale School closed in 1964, a year after I left it, and Skelwith Bridge in 1970. Chapel Stile School, the lifeblood of the community, continues with some 48 pupils. The local economy now depends principally on tourism.

ABOVE LEFT: The rock art at Langdale Boulders takes a number of different forms; concentric rings connected by straight lines are dominant here. No one to date has been able to interpret the meaning of these markings, though part of the image here looks uncannily to me like a three-wheeled bike!

ABOVE: Langdale axes come in many different sizes. Two enormous axe head roughings, approximately 60 centimetres (2 feet) long, were until recently used as door stops at the Old Dungeon Ghyll Hotel, when it was run by Sid and Jammy Cross. Any axes found these days should be left in situ and their location reported (with a map reference) to a Lake District National Park or National Trust Warden.

summer

It rains – has it ever been this wet before? When the sun breaks through it's hay time in the fields. The whole valley becomes green like nowhere else. Then it's warm, and you can swim in the pool below Slaters Bridge and upstream in Rob's Hole. Climbers watch the sun go down from the blood-red rhyolite of Gimmer Crag. Thirsty walkers head for the excellent hostelries that grace the Langdales. Swallows swoop across the fields. Bats stream out at dusk.

OPPOSITE: Moonrise from Pike o' Blisco.

LEFT: Between the cam stones on the sunny top of a stone wall near Low Hallgarth a little ecosystem flourishes. Different mosses and lichens are complemented by the tiny flowers of saxifrage.

OPPOSITE: The farmsteads of Low and High Hallgarth, overlooking Little Langdale Tarn, are thought to have been built in the early 1600s and retain many of their original features. Now owned by the National Trust, they provide permanent accommodation for a family working in the area, a 'rest hut' for a long-standing climbing club and a variety of holiday lets.

OVERLEAF: The ravine of Megs Gill rises from Walthwaite, a kind of 'suburb' of Chapel Stile. To the right is Raven Crag. The annual Langdale Gala fell race starts in the fields at the bottom left. The runners climb to the left of the crag to the skyline, then loop round to descend on the right. I stand in Walthwaite shouting invaluable encouragement.

ABOVE: The slate-roofed stone farms, cottages and inns of the Langdales are in perfect harmony with their surroundings. No need for grandiose design, state-of-the-art technology or award-winning architecture – practical experience and use of the natural materials to hand have produced buildings that are good both to live in and to look at.

Blea Tarn House (top left) is sometimes known as Solitary because of its secluded position above both Langdales.

Attached to the farm of Stang End is this neat little cottage (top right): it faces (unseen in this photograph) a stone barn with a traditional spinning gallery – a real Lakeland feature.

The hamlet of Hodge Close has a pretty cottage (bottom left) opposite the old smithy that once served the nearby slate quarry.

Little Langdale's Three Shires Inn (bottom right), once called The Traveller's Rest, is known to locals as Low Jerry.

ABOVE: A perfect summer's day in the centre of Little Langdale valley. The bracken is green on Lingmoor and the grass is ready for cutting in the meadows.

OPPOSITE: The peregrine falcon is Britain's fastest predator: it can dive in a 'stoop' at something like 240 m.p.h. – a wonderful sight.

OPPOSITE INSET: A hen peregrine feeds her three chicks on a Langdale crag – keeping a beady eye on the photographer suspended on a rope opposite! In the 1960s my father was licensed by the Nature Conservancy to mark peregrine eggs to make them valueless to collectors. He used to lower me on a rope to their nests, and I have had a love affair with them ever since. Virtually my first photograph, taken when I was eight, was of peregrine chicks.

ABOVE: An immature kestrel surveys the valley below for mouse or beetle. The commonest of the Lakeland falcons, which include merlin and peregrine, its hovering flight and attractive reddish brown plumage make it the easiest of the group to identify.

ABOVE INSET: I came across these beautiful red-brown kestrel eggs while making a rock climb on a remote crag. They were nestling on a rock ledge in a neatly formed basin of dead grass. I quickly left the scene so as not to disturb the parents in their task of hatching.

OPPOSITE: Looking to the flanks of Lingmoor above the bend in the Great Langdale valley, a thousand shades of green mark a Langdale summer.

BELOW: Crinkle Crags viewed from Pike o' Blisco. Long Top, the highest crinkle, forms the centrepiece; from here steep scree tumbles into the depths of Crinkle Gill. A direct traverse from the first Crinkle, seen to the left, to Long Top involves negotiation of the notorious 'bad step' – a rocky scramble of 4.5 metres (15 feet). The name 'Crinkle' was originally thought to be a simple description of the skyline silhouette of the crags, but recently it has been suggested that it comes from the Old Norse 'kringla', meaning a circle: take your pick.

OVERLEAF: Running due south from the centre of Little Langdale, a secretive wooded corridor cuts through the hills to Tilberthwaite and then on to Yewdale and the Vale of Coniston. From a high vantage point on Lingmoor, this view looks through the end of that corridor to the head of Coniston Lake. Thankfully the track is rough and unsuitable for cars, keeping the area a quiet haven for walkers. Slate quarries delineate the valley on each side.

BELOW: Haymaking carries
on apace in Langdale beneath
the watch of the Pikes. Once a
heavy shower of rain or a sudden
thunderstorm could ruin the hay.
Now it is mostly sealed inside
large plastic bags and it doesn't
matter if they get wet.

ancient traces

There are many signs of prehistory in the Langdales. The most visible and widely known is the Neolithic stone axe 'factory' on the Pikes. Stone engravings on the boulders have recently been officially recognised as an important piece of the jigsaw; other rock markings in Langdale have yet to be declared. There are also remnants of the Bronze Age in the form of burial mounds and hut circles – many of these, too, are still undocumented.

In more modern times, the Romans most certainly built a road through Little Langdale – and they lived there, too. One could hardly imagine anyone passing through without wanting to stay! Farms and houses have come and gone; many stones are still set in the ground to mark their passing even if little or nothing is known of their history and origins.

The Vikings held their parliament at the Ting Mound behind what is now Fell Foot Farm. My grandfather, when he wanted, used to speak a language that went way beyond heavy dialect and was virtually Old Norse. He found it very useful for talking to the local vicar, who couldn't understand a word. When I was at school all the farm lads still counted sheep in what is probably a mixture of Norse and Celtic.

RIGHT: If you want to stay awake, count sheep in the traditional Lakeland manner. There are a number of variations; the Langdale version, from one to ten, goes: yan, taen, tethera, methera, pimp, sethera, lethera, hovera, dovera, dick. Notice that the fifth and tenth words have a rather crude connotation!

OPPOSITE TOP: On Blea Moss Common at the head of Little Langdale is this group of stones which locals call 'the Little Langdale stone circle'. At first it is easy to dismiss it as a walled enclosure for animals, making use of two large boulders, now in ruins. But look again: part of the wall is of double-skinned stone, sunk into the present ground level. It closely resembles the construction of other embanked stone circles found in Furness and on Moor Divock. Nearby, often hidden behind a cloak of bracken, lies what is probably a multi-chambered burial mound. A possible date for the site is early Bronze Age, c. 2,000 BC.

OPPOSITE CENTRE: This benched earth mound is the site of the Viking Ting (parliament), one of the best preserved outside Iceland. Until relatively recent times, it was a revered local feature kept in pristine condition.

ABOVE: Looking over Langdale Boulders to the Pikes in midsummer, the undersides of the oak leaves are revealed as the wind whips up the clouds. The site has been adopted by English Heritage and the markings on the boulders rated among the most important prehistoric rock art in Europe. The San people of Africa, whose incredible fine line paintings in the Western Cape date to at least 6,000 years of age, left a song that evokes a sentiment that could equally be applied to the Langdale art:

'The day we die
a soft wind will blow away our
    footprints in the sand.
When the wind has gone
Who will tell the timelessness
That once we walked this way
    in the dawn of time?'

work and play

Tourism and conservation

Tourists started to visit the Langdale valleys in the mid-eighteenth century – gentlemen of letters and artists who initially made much of the 'horror' of the crags and the 'dreadful heights'. This fear soon turned into a more balanced appreciation of the true beauty of the region. Father West wrote the first guide for tourists in 1778, and soon the trickle of visitors became a flood. In the nineteenth century, artists were keen to capture the beauty of the Langdales and the drama of the Pikes, in particular. Wordsworth wrote the final version of his best-selling Guide to the Lakes in 1835. Along with the opening of Windermere Station in 1847, this had a far-reaching effect on tourism in Langdale. The improvement of the roads and the advance of the motor-car were the next boost. Today some twelve million tourists visit the Lake District National Park each year, and a significant number of these – around a million a year – tour the Langdales.

In 1951 the Lake District became a National Park, which served to control development and conserve the landscape. Another major influence protecting the environment is that the landowner who controls most of the farms throughout the two valleys is the National Trust, set up as a charity to acquire property – specifically 'places of historic interest or natural beauty' – with the aim of protecting these for the public benefit. The Friends of the Lake District is another protective body that does much good work for the Langdales.

Both the National Park Authority and the National Trust, assisted with able teams of volunteers, have set about repairing footpaths over the fells. The stamping of many feet has taken its toll, particularly over recent years, and this has been a big exercise in conservation. Despite a feeling of intrusion into special places, this hard work does seem to be reducing the overall visual and environmental impact of people using the fells.

Walking and climbing

Research in the aftermath of the 2001 foot-and-mouth epidemic, during which public access to the hills was banned by law, has shown that by far the greatest contributors to the economy of the Langdales are those using the fells to climb and walk. Banning access, for whatever reason, dealt a severe financial blow to the area.

Fell use by walkers and climbers started with the birth of tourism. To enjoy the full beauty of the region you simply have to go on foot. Increasingly large numbers now do so, and a network of favourite walks and paths, often using ancient ways and passes, has grown up.

The first recorded climb took place on Pavey Ark in around 1870, when Richard Pendlebury, Professor of Mathematics at Cambridge, early Alpinist and pioneer of British rock climbing, ascended Jack's Rake and left a note in the visitor's book at the Old Dungeon Ghyll Hotel to the effect that it was 'a striking yet simple excursion among magnificent rock scenery'. Undoubtedly local shepherds had made use of the natural diagonal fault that soars across the crag for centuries. Nevertheless, this marked a beginning and acted as a spur to others. An ascent of South-East Gully on Gimmer Crag was recorded in 1896, and the great Bowfell Buttress was first climbed in 1902, a major landmark in the history of Langdale climbing.

Many have subsequently contributed to the development of rock climbing in the Langdales, but the first local person to make a significant impact on the climbing scene, raising the standard of difficulty to new heights, was a quarryman from Little Langdale: my father, Jim Birkett. I have made my own contribution, but the mantle has recently been taken up by Dave Birkett, Jim's grandson, who has moved Langdale rock climbing to an awesome level of difficulty.

Weather and the seasons

While global warming is now accepted as a scientific fact, weather patterns and the seasons have always varied between considerable extremes in the Langdales. Some clear sunny winter days can be much warmer and pleasanter than those to be had in summer and vice versa. Snow can be prevalent in both spring and autumn.

In the big winter freeze of 1962–3, all the tarns and lakes froze solid and on most days the children of Little Langdale played ice hockey on the tarn. Mains electricity had not reached the valley at this date, so the long cold nights turned into a shivering marathon. They seemed to go on for ever.

The endless hot summer of 1976 produced drought conditions, but summers can be contrary here. Ten years earlier, on 13 August 1966, the Langdales were hit by the worst storm in living memory. *The Westmorland Gazette* reported it thus:

> A violent thunderstorm following 12 hours of incessant rain produced a night of terror in the Langdale valley. Half-a-dozen mountain streams, swollen to fierce torrents, burst their banks, sweeping away stone walls and parts of the road. The flood waters raged through two hotels, farms and several houses and inundated the National Trust camping site at the head of the valley. The onrush tore away parts of the fellsides and turned Elterwater and the northern reaches of Lake Windermere brown. As they receded on Sunday, the scene at the head of the valley was of devastation.

The climate of the Langdales is dominated by Atlantic air currents and the Gulf Stream, which generally produce mild winters and cool summers. But the rules for weather and seasonal behaviour here are simple: there are none. In truth, the high fells apart, the number of wet days is not substantially greater in the Langdales than in the rest of England. But that is not to say that the rain here isn't heavier!

Farming today

Lakeland hill farming is thought by many to be an idyllic life, with man caring for his flock against the raw elements of the mountains. The real state of hill farming today does not quite fit this image. A combination of the way Langdale hill farmers receive their money through subsidies and the development of modern technologies has produced a situation that is not environmentally friendly. Yet despite the huge cost to the taxpayer of the disasters of 'mad cow disease' and the foot-and-mouth epidemic, little or nothing has changed.

There are many problems. Increased hill flocks and massive overgrazing is one – helicopters are now used to carry food supplements to the high fells. Flower diversity is being eaten away and vegetation cover reduced to such an extent that serious erosion is taking place. Poisoning of the watercourses by the chemicals used to dip sheep is another. When I was a boy all the becks in the Langdales were full of brown trout; there is now hardly a sign of them. Heavy machinery and new technology over-compact the land and smash lanes and farmyards to pieces. Great piles of plastic bags, like rubbish dumps in the middle of the National Park, have replaced the traditional way of haymaking. New barns of wood and concrete are being thrown up, while traditional stone barns become redundant.

Of course, a good number of farmers care for their land and recognise the problems. With the right political and financial incentives, many would return to a more environmentally sensitive and caring way of farming. At Wilson Place Farm in Little Langdale John and Maureen Birkett look after a number of Sites of Special Scientific Interest, and at Millbeck Farm in Great Langdale Eric Taylforth has shunned the use of chemicals to produce lamb and beef of high quality, which he sells direct from the farm. I applaud their efforts.

autumn

Fruit is picked. Leaves colour magnificently and conkers fall from the tree. The days shorten. Tups are put in with the ewes. Birds and animals disappear. Fingers feel cold and hands are stuffed into pockets; silly hats are pulled down over the ears. Sticks are piled high and bonfires lit. Suddenly, one morning, the tops have turned ghostly white. The first snows of winter have arrived.

OPPOSITE: Blackberries – along with mushrooms, raspberries, hazelnuts, slough berries, elderberries, sweet chestnuts and crab apples – make the wild harvest of autumn a children's paradise. The best things in life are free – if you can put up with the occasional stomach-ache, that is!

OVERLEAF: Sunrise over Little Langdale Tarn – which is hidden down there somewhere beneath the mist.

BELOW: The maple tree in the centre of the village of Elterwater is golden-yellow, with a hint of green still lingering behind the outer canopy. But a sharp frost followed by a stiff breeze could leave only a skeleton by tomorrow. Exactly when the best autumn colours will materialise is a fickle business to predict. As a rule of thumb, late October almost leading into November is best – but don't blame me if you arrive to find all the leaves have been stripped bare.

OPPOSITE: This view down from Lingmoor, with the leaves just beginning to turn, reveals that Elterwater is in fact three distinct basins. The Great Langdale Beck enters the last downstream basin, issuing beneath Rob Rash Wood. Visual evidence, however, indicates that this beck once emptied into the middle basin, as does the River Brathay from Little Langdale. The beck is now obviously flowing down a man-made channel, with constructed banks on either side: did it perhaps once follow a completely different course, one that led directly to the head of the upper basin (below what is now Eltermere Hotel)?

ABOVE: Looking down to Side Pike from Pike o' Blisco early on a bright autumn morning, you may catch the cloud still lingering in Great Langdale.

94

ABOVE: Mickleden's rich green mosaic of stone wall and field contrasts with the first dusting of snow on the heights of Bowfell. Seen from the pass to Blea Tarn, Oxendale lies in the shadow of Pike o' Blisco and Kettle Crag.

LEFT: Honey Fungus, shown here growing near Slaters Bridge, is reputedly edible although I have never tried it – the traditional Langdale attitude to mushrooms other than the straightforward field or horse mushroom is to leave well alone. That may be a pity because in autumn the Langdales produce a varied crop – for the discerning these include the yellow Chanterelle, Penny Buns, Chicken in the Woods and Puffball. Have a care, however: the Death Cap also grows here (actually in the grounds of Langdale School!) – it is fatally poisonous and has no known antidote or cure.

BELOW: Early autumn down Greenburn Beck towards Little Langdale Tarn shows the bracken already rusting to a rich red-brown. The footbridge closes the circuit of the classic Greenburn Horseshoe, which rounds Greenburn over the tops of Wetherlam, Swirl How and the Carrs to join the descent from Wetside Edge with a track rising from the valley to Greenburn mines. The mining of malachite (green copper ore) caused discoloration of the water, giving the burn (the word is Celtic) its name. The dark fell dominant in the central background is Red Screes.

OVERLEAF: Over High Bield to Little Langdale Tarn, the sun melts the frost to show the green beneath. A few leaves linger, but snow is beginning to coat the high tops.

BELOW: Slaters Bridge is a favourite spot for many people. Some speculate that the narrow arch of the bridge may be of Roman origin. Although the main east–west Roman road – from Port Ravenglass to Ambleside via the spectacular Hardknott Fort – went over Wrynose Pass and through the valley, I don't think there is any hard evidence to support this theory. Undoubtedly the simply supported slate flags that span the rest of the River Brathay are from relatively modern quarrying (certainly within the last four hundred years!).

OPPOSITE: A perfectly proportioned oak tree frames the view to Fell Foot Farm. The farm, at the very foot of Wrynose Pass, is distinguished by a secret porch at the front, used to transfer illicit whiskey distilled by Lanty Slee. The Ting Mound (site of the Viking parliament) is at the back.

ABOVE: Over Bridge End to the
Pikes, clouds gather in the hills
and cast a shadow over the
junipers of Blea Moss. The
lines of trees trace three becks:
Greenburn passing Bridge End;
Wrynose passing Fell Foot, and
Blea Moss passing beneath
the road courtesy of Puff Low
(pronounced to rhyme with
sow) Bridge.

ABOVE: From the summit cairn on Wetherlam the views in all directions are exceptional. Here we are looking north: Pike o' Blisco, Crinkle Crags and Bowfell are on the centre skyline, the Scafells are to the left and the solitary Pike o' Stickle to the right.

OVERLEAF: Reflections in Red Tarn catch Great Knott, the Crinkles and Bowfell in the absolute stillness of a perfect autumnal dawn. Towards the edge of the basin, just before it drops into Oxendale down Browney Gill, stands a photographer with a medium-format camera on a tripod. Can you spot him? I hope he got a good shot!

ABOVE: Looking towards Bowfell
from Side Pike, a ruined stone
wall sets off a scene of high
contrast – white snows on the
tops, dark shadows in Mickleden.

ABOVE: The plucky cone of Side Pike above Blea Tarn House makes for a good little excursion from the top of Blea Tarn Pass. It offers fine views over the heads of both Langdales.

LEFT: Blea Tarn on a wild and blustery day is just as awe-inspiring as in stillness.

markers

BELOW LEFT: Three Shires Stone at the head of Wrynose Pass is a good spot from which to commence a traverse of the Crinkles. Marking the meeting of the old counties of Westmorland, Lancashire and Cumberland, it is made of limestone and bears the inscription 'WF 1816' on the back, although it was not erected until some time after this date. Broken into three pieces, it was glued back together in 1997 with much pomp and ceremony, and modern stones placed round it to depict the positions of the old counties. They needn't have bothered: 'Cumberland' was already written out large in stone on the hillside nearby!

BELOW: The Neddy Boggle Stone at Elterwater Common. A boggle is a ghost: this innocent-looking marker stone has a reputation for spooking horses. Many's the time that horse and pony have refused to pass or instead have bolted by. Another strange thing: do you notice how the top of the stone fits directly into the profile of Harrison Stickle and Pavey Ark silhouetted behind?

OPPOSITE TOP: The distinctive beehive-shaped Swirl How summit cairn marks one of the high tops of the southern fells. Marker cairns have been built on the Langdale fells for many years, probably thousands. Not very far from this one, my son found a perfectly formed flint arrowhead, about the size of a fingernail.

OPPOSITE BOTTOM: Encrusted with the cold fingers of rime ice, this simple wooden cross is found at the head of Greenburn, on the col known as Broad Slack between Swirl How and Great Carrs. It marks the site where, on the stormy night of 22 October 1944, a Royal Canadian Air Force Halifax 'S For Sugar' failed to clear the heights of Broad Slack and crashed, killing all crew.

index